THE AUTUMN MYTH

THE AUTUMN MYTH
Joel Lane

PUBLICATIONS
2010

Published by Arc Publications
Nanholme Mill, Shaw Wood Road
Todmorden OL14 6DA, UK
www.arcpublications.co.uk

Copyright © Joel Lane, 2010
Design by Tony Ward
Printed in Great Britain by the
MPG Book Group, Bodmin & King's Lynn

978 1904614 76 0 pbk
978 1906570 16 3 hbk

ACKNOWLEDGEMENTS:

Thanks are due to the editors of the following publications, in
which some of these poems first appeared:
*Acumen, Ambit, and maybe do a dance or two, Chimera, Dream Catcher,
Equinox, The Interpreter's House, Iota, Lamport Court, Other Poetry,
Rain Dog, Raw Edge, The Rialto, Smiths Knoll, Stand, Staple,
Under the Radar, Urban District Writers.*

Thanks are also due to the following for their help, advice and
encouragement: Simon Bestwick, Julie Boden, John Clarke, Jane
Commane, Gul Davis, Steve Green, John Howard, Ella Lane, Des
Lewis, Gary McMahon, Chris Morgan, Christina Morris, Matt
Nunn, Kate Pearce, Jacqui Rowe, Mick Scully, Julie Wilson.

Cover illustration: Marcus Ward.

*For Simon Bestwick,
a valued companion
on the midnight train*

Supported by
ARTS COUNCIL
ENGLAND

Editor for the UK and Ireland: John W. Clarke

CONTENTS

ONE

THE REFUGEE

The last thing you expected to find
in a carrier bag, on a skip:
a human skull. The police told you
it had been part of a teenage girl.
No trace of skin or hair, no DNA
to link it to a family, a name,
a face anyone could remember.
She had no story to be doubted,
no marks of possible self-harm.

The first thing you noticed, holding up
its yellow cheekbones to the rain,
was how it smiled. As if it knew
its passport could not be revoked.
It had found the way out of trouble:
dropped from the news into science,
taken its place among rocks and stars.

SUITABLE FOR VIEWING

The children laugh as their mother plays
piano, and their uncles dance.
A warm firelight paints their faces
with a harmless fever. They are safe.
But the screen itself is howling.

The lovers pull the thick curtains
to shut out the hotel courtyard,
and kneel face to face on the bed
at the window of each other's flesh.
But the screen itself is crying.

The survivors, the reprieved, the thankful
pour from their barricaded houses
into streets where no shadow hangs.
Lovers hold hands. Children sing.
But the screen itself is ashes.

THE MANDATE

As the first ripples of the crowd's laughter
struck the air like a window breaking
to let in a fresh autumn breeze,
the Emperor lifted a bare arm
and slowly wiped away a tear.
"Oh child," he said gently, "if only
you knew how much strength that laughter
gives to the enemies of our nation.
Laugh, child, laugh. I weep for you
and for us all." The laughter died
as if someone had tripped a switch.
The boy looked around, dumbstruck.
Many hands reached out for him
as bottles were smashed, stones picked up.

Three days later, the Emperor was returned
to power by a safe majority.
The swearing-in ceremony was broadcast
so the nation could see a proud man
building on his past, wearing cloth
to cover his nipples, cock and arse:
thin strips of some pale fabric
so pure, so delicate, it could almost
have been the skin of a child.

RED BASTARDS

Go in early, get it done and leave.
We've been worried about this estate
at the northern corner of the city,
but it's an incandescent Sunday morning

and the glow reflects from the concrete
to print our skins with unity.
As we trot from door to door and post
copies of *Searchlight*, a thin man

watches us. He tears up the paper.
"Do you want it?" he says. "The firm
will be here in five minutes." He pokes
at his mobile, starts talking hard.

One of us wants to stay and fight.
He's outvoted. They've been known
to use paving slabs. We drive away.
I think about the last time:

the glob of spit on the car window
still gleaming as we left the district,
our voices rising above the situation
while the fear waited down below

to unfold its many legs and crawl
up into my chest, an insect larva
already at the awkward age,
impossible to evict or live with.

REQUEST

A minute's silence. That's all.
It takes longer to clean your teeth,
much longer to have your photo taken.
I'm sure you can find a minute.
What might be more difficult, perhaps,
is finding that much silence.

Let me help you.
There was your silence when we asked
why the dead weren't counted.
There was your silence when the proof
was exposed as a legend,
when the dead were exposed as dead,
the severed limbs as missing.

Why not dub some of that in?
All that footage. That blank tape of you.

COLONIAL DREAMS

You see them, from time to time, in hotels
or drinking clubs. Old, stiff-backed,
their heads moving from side to side
as if scanning a distant horizon.

They were young in a world of borders
where drunken men muttered the facts
about life, explained what women were,
what dark rivers flowed under the skin.

They scanned the relief map of their needs:
this country was discipline, that was pain.
They walked through the fever-trees, alone,
to the sour cave by the river of plasma.

When the foreign upstarts took control
of the colonists' birthright, they came home
to find the same heat disguised as winter –
the same mouths open, the same skin

needing punishment, the lessons to be taught
in prisons, detention centres, asylums.
Divide and rule. But the world healed up
behind your back, then came after you –

and so they end up like this, red-eyed,
backs to a wall where damp has grown
a strange forest, dividing the blank future
with alcohol and fear, colonising themselves.

SLOW FADE

What did you do
when the future was dying?
I watched the shadows fall like decay
across newspapers and streets
that had never held the truth.
They were all soaked in petrol;
one match and they'd go up.

What did you do
when the future was dying?
I joined a self-help group
to improve my relationships,
talked through my family history,
got a long-term prescription
to stop me harming myself.

What did you do
when the future was dying?
I deconstructed the innocent,
found them compromised like me,
strange bedfellows, not my kind.
I burned their passports in my head
and told myself, *nobody belongs*.

What did you do
when the future was dying?
I marched with the others.
The papers dismissed us
as living in another world.
They said the future was a criminal
and by then, I couldn't disagree.

COME BACK NEXT YEAR
for Tove Jansson

Every winter, as the iris of night
widens at something behind you,
a lost tune creeps through your head.
Pine trees bristle on the hillside

where the wanderer in his pointed hat
walks across the frozen river,
playing his mouth organ, unheard,
while his friends sleep underground.

In the distance, clouds are glowing,
and the wind from the mountains
smells like the sky has gone bad.
He stops, turns, then starts to run

past the iron trees, the blank walls
topped with razor-wire. An echo
imitates his cry. He falls, gets up,
starts to look for a hiding-place.

TABULA RASA

The ants did their slow, deliberate work,
swarming over the head like points of ink,
obsessive as journalists, thorough as police.

First to go was the neatly severed neck,
then the bruised mouth, the torn eyelids,
the vocal cords raw from screaming.

The ants poured like a river of years
to bleach the contamination of flesh away
from the hard, vacant skull of a fanatic.

A DREAM DEFUELLED
after Langston Hughes

These are the fractions of oil
separated in a refinery:
tar, diesel, petrol, kerosene.
The waste products are burned off.

We simmer in our homes, afraid
of an army of hidden faces.
The roadway stinks of petrol,
the newspapers stink of petrol.

The blood-red flowers excrete
their fumes into your mind.
You drive to the border and swear.
"This is about defending freedom."

What becomes of humanity
when it's soaked in crude oil?
Does it go up in flames, like paper?
Or does it just spoil?

THE AUTUMN MYTH

Nobody's bought a skull mask.
There never was an October
like van Gogh's avenue of fire,
a slow and ecstatic decay –

only this *Daily Mail* exposure
of what we all knew, the days
brief and unexpectedly warm,
the nights bitter. All at once

the trees are stripped and searched
and the gloves thrown away.
The only autumn's in your head:
the slow dissolution of childhood

as Parliament fails to blow up,
and on every bare-knuckled street
fireworks slam again and again
like the doors of some vast institution.

INTERNAL SECURITY

It's my job to take care of the leopard.
I'm the keeper, the warden, the man with the key.
It's my job to keep his claws filed down
and cut his food into mouthable shreds.

He won't challenge me. He knows who's boss.
And if he forgets, I've got a rifle.
It's my job to enter his cage at night
and break his shin-bones with a rock hammer.

Our safety guaranteed, I go back to writing
my book on the leopard's genetic defects:
how it's not equipped by nature to run,
how its claws are merely vestigial.

SAFE PASSAGE

Nobody wants any trouble. The backstreets
around Holloway Head are clear.
No drunks, drug dealers, or girls
pretending to wait for taxis.
No drivers making the slow trawl
through the shallow waters of midnight.

But in five minutes you've passed
half a dozen gentlemen's clubs,
two sauna and massage parlours.
Small factories, recently converted.
Businessmen and travelling reps
come here for a touch of the outside.

This is where refugees end up.
Behind tinted or shuttered windows
the limits of Europe are exposed.
Wherever you walk on the blameless street,
you are no more than nine yards
and one wall from a naked woman.

THE HOUSE OF LIES

One long table seats us all, twelve
ex-rebels at a reunion dinner.
The talk is of children, travel, new jobs,
and no-one has much to drink.
Like an extended family, we take
the ashes of the past for granted.
No need to re-shout the anger,
re-cry the tears. This isn't the pub.
We fought for years, and we lost.
There's little talk of the company:

the preening managers, their suits
coated with the snail-tracks of lies,
presiding over the cost-effective stone
of a car park that was an office;
the gollum clones of Human Resources
hiding behind computers, their lies
the vaseline on the broomstick;
the overdressed dogfish of sales
with their spreadsheets and PowerPoint
ten-minute presentations of lies;

the lying appraisals, the sycophants
planted in meetings to repeat lies,
the less than candid press releases,
the way the aircon began to smell
of lies – a smell like old banknotes
picked out of the gutter and dried
but not rinsed, before being spent –

the quarterly lies, the sales conference lies,
the special lies told to the union,
the 'home truths', the realpolitik, the lies.

But not you, my friends. It wasn't you
whose words poisoned the air.
We fought in the meeting room, we
fought through the union, we fought
at our desks. We were shafted.
It's time to go. Most of us
don't live round here any more.
We kiss goodbye on the pavement,
feeling suddenly lost, out of time,
choked with an old and alien truth.

URBAN POSTCARDS

The Cut

Starting in Digbeth, the canal walkway
extends four miles, a grey bandage
unravelled along the thighbone
of a dead patient, and ends

between a cemetery and a hospital
in Yardley. It lies there
unhealed, out of commission,
waiting for the city to join it.

Longbridge

The gates are open. Traffic
pauses on the dual carriageway
as the workers leave, hours
after the usual day-shift;

thousands of silent figures
crossing the road, no-one
looking back. As if to stop
would mean being wiped out.

Black Country

A photo in the evening paper
of fascists punching the air,
their cry of rage and triumph
preserved at full volume;

three days later, a slogan
painted white on a factory wall
gave me this formless headache
like someone else's hangover.

Tornado

A tilted funnel of darkness
and rain, a late-summer freak,
it ripped a bloody passage
out through the city's thorax –

unable to drop its own rage
the way it dropped cars or people,
it stumbled, fell to its knees,
left a scar the shape of itself.

Lee Bank

This estate is a place to hide
drugs, hide stolen goods, or just hide.
Tarpaulins are hoods for shattered
windows, screams no-one can hear.

Decay isolates the tower blocks
in their long wait for demolition;
the only way to mend the damage
is to tear them down and start again.

Stained

In the shadow of the flyovers
and tower blocks, the old streets
of North Birmingham are drowning
as the water table shifts up

through brick and woodwork,
through the roar of traffic.
It's too late for a spray job,
for *not in front of the kids*.

The Swan

It's not the way the two pale towers
stare each other out, either side
of the Swan Centre, or the roar
of the traffic beneath your feet;

it's something you don't recognise
that pushes you down – all around you,
rising from the grey pavement,
the shadows of an inverted world.

Eclipse

The light cannot get a hold
on the Hyatt's mirrored wall,
the smoked windows of limousines
outside the lap-dancing clubs,

the steel shutter that coffins
an empty bookshop. It burns
in the frozen air, like money,
and leaves no trace behind.

SINK

In 2006, Birmingham City Council refused to make a donation to the building of a museum in Wales to commemorate the villages flooded half a century ago when the reservoirs from which Birmingham obtains its water were constructed.

The skyline is a used blade:
what might have been fertile
is a shaven cleft we drink from.

Who needs a museum
for the lost towns? Their salts
whiten our sceptical teeth.

Go ahead, cry in the water:
gaze down at the blurred streets
where couples embrace or fight,

swearing in a dead language.
Get a job, boyo, get a bath;
we just don't do the past.

28

BOSS HOUSE

Just here, where the road narrows
and what used to be a grass verge
is a fenced-off domain of trenches;
where, at night, the streetlamps
don't quite reveal the way.
Opposite the Boss House Hotel.

Here in broad daylight, a boy
stalked you – his friends watching
from the hotel's front yard –
to smack you hard from behind
on the right ear, knocking you down.
Then he walked away, unhidden.

And it's just here that you pause,
look behind you, then check
your ID. For the bank, of course –
not because, here, you're passing
through a zone where you don't belong,
where your papers are not in order.

CLOSED

The woman on the stage
freezes in a mime of shock.
Her voice is cut down
by the applause of bricks
smashing the plate-glass windows.

Later, the elders declare
a victory for their faith.
The circle of silence
spreads outwards, like oil,
from the unlit theatre.

TWO

--

THE MESCAL WORM

Look carefully, and you'll see me
curled up in the end of the bottle
like some piss artist's hallucination.

I am a dragon in embryo,
and my raw flesh secretes dreams.
All flavour is a dilute poison.

I am the bitterness that starts fires,
shatters glass, turns over the tables,
fills casualty wards. I'm not buying.

My blood is the stain of a child
whose pieces were buried long ago
in the forest, and never dug up.

My flesh sets your teeth on edge,
colder than the ice in your drink.
I taste bad. But I won't kill you.

FREEZE-OUT

You used to keep a glass paperweight
on the desk where you wrote your books.
Now and then, in a thoughtful way,
you'd shake it to watch the pale flakes
swirl in chaos and then settle
over the little house. But one night

you shook the paperweight so hard
the snow never did stop drifting,
and the man looked out the window
to see the snow dissolving the glass
and swirling through, touching his face,
while the woman looked in the mirror

to see nothing but a blizzard
filling the room, making the house white
like her smile. And the glass frosted,
then shattered – and the paperweight
was only a fine layer of splinters
over your keyboard, papers, chair.

That's what I found in the study,
but when I came to the kitchen
you said: "Don't fret, that isn't glass.
It's just snow. Forget the desk, boy,
nothing good ever happens there.
The bedroom is where the real work

gets done. Have I ever told you
how good I am in bed?"
And for the next two hours,
you told me how good you were.
But strangely (given my track record),
I didn't ask you to show me.

THE RITUALS

Not every night, or every weekend,
but now and then without warning
he twisted her arm behind her back

and beat her naked body with his belt
until her blood stained the duvet.
And afterwards, he held her still

and stroked her diminished face,
kissed the blue-black runes that stood
like Braille on her damp skin,

matched her breathing with his own
and quietened his own terror in her.
They had two children, both madness.

LEGENDS

The General was an older brother to her
as time slowly robbed her of peers.
She went ballistic when he was placed
under arrest, declared the prison unworthy
to hold a man of his stature. She backed up
the myth of paralysis he acted out –
and when he flew home, she cracked open
the best champagne for the cameras.

It cost her, though. The bottle soon
had control, and her doctors advised her
to make no more public appearances.
She sat in her guarded home, bleached
to driftwood by age and thirst,
wetting her dry lips with stories
of punishments the General had used
to make them be silent, or speak.

Further down the bottle, not floating
but shrunken and pale, was the image
of herself at sixteen when she'd dated
the local bully, so she could watch
the lessons he gave to the weaker boys
and, bending her head close, hear
the filthy confessions his hands choked
from their writhing blue lips.

Blue Town

Rain taps out its fast, intimate rhythm
on cramped terraces and bony streets.
The scene looks cold, but it isn't.

Around us, the hills crouch like dogs.
We follow the thread of a sobbing
harmonica, let the chords pull us

to where a slate-grey Pennine town
woke up this morning, transformed.
A paraffin flame dances with me.

Three days of rhythm, laced with the smoke
of whisky, blues and lack of sleep,
you in my hands like a guitar.

UNPLUGGED

As the storm hit the mountain-side,
the silent musicians in the tour bus
began to scream recriminations –

not getting through to each other
as rain shattered the blank windows.
You were holding me, stroking my face,

saying a name I didn't recognise.
When I surfaced, an empty cage,
you were the only real thing.

We talked. We kissed in the night
while far below, the tour bus
plunged into icy feedback.

SOME OF THESE DAYS

She was flavour of the decade,
the little redhead who acted out
Judy and Shirley with a shy grin
and the rhythm of a marching band:

hands rolling, throat full out,
giving it everything she'd got,
eyes bigger than her child's belly
and swollen with reflected light.

The repeats kept her famous
while she pared herself down
in music college, then a clinic.
At the perfect age to launch

a glittering career, she starved
and no contracts could feed her.
The empty click of shutters
kept her awake every night.

Her last recorded performance
was nobody's magic moment:
the bones showed in her arms
and her face was translucent,

her eyes vast with darkness.
The song was old, but not faked.
I've swallowed a camera. Now
it's eating me from the inside.

HOMESICK
Maryport, 2006

Homesick James, born in Tennessee
and the oldest Chicago bluesman,
is helped onto the bare stage
and guided to his stool,
where they strap on his guitar
and fix his microphone.

After eighty years of playing
slide guitar, he needs an amp
to get his strength back.
The audience are restless.
"I'm gonna play," he says,
"you listen if you want."

His first note cuts
the night cleanly in half.

REPOSSESSED

His smile drove a generation
to the youth clubs, the discos,
through the ceiling of a room
wallpapered with his face;

the five boys, their passion
covered by guitars, their necks
wrapped in tartan scarves;
they brought a cold ecstasy

to those unready for it.
After years of being treated
like angels with golden cocks
and nothing under their haircuts

but an absence that sang,
they grew up. And split up.
As if by magic, his money
vanished. The house he'd bought

for his parents was repossessed.
Thirty years later, that still hurt.
I wish you'd fucked me literally.
It would have been easier.

He still makes a living
from the god he once was,
but the footage has broken up:
only a collection of stills.

Take a little love
still echoes in my gut
and my eyes, like his, drop
to the flame no lyric mentions.

THE SACRED COAST

Towards dawn, you gave up
trying to sleep. You left her side
and walked down to the quay
where the gulls introduced you

to an audience of dark boats
huddled under tarpaulins
like a sullen festival crowd.
The retreating tide made visible

the empty bottles, the smashed
wineglasses, torn-up plastic
food cartons, things discarded
like outtakes from a bad session;

the waves rippling like casual applause
in the broken window of sunlight.
Under it all, the slow endless drag:
the boats straining to get away

but in the end, not really bothered.
To hear the breath of the world
in your own cold harbour
does not always feel good.

NERUDA

The night air is as heavy as rush hour traffic.
She opens a window, clears away
the empty wine-bottle. She is singing
but has no idea what song it is.

He looks up from the table, his jaw
darkening with stubble. "It's finished,"
he says, gives her the blue notebook.
She stands by the window to read it

in the dual light of moon and bulb.
Her eyes are tired. The words burn
from the curling pages like smoke.
She puts the notebook down carefully

on the ledge, turns to face him.
Two minutes later, rain is beating
against the windows like a flock
of trapped pigeons. Lightning flares

and waves of nausea shake the road.
They don't care. They are at it like cats
on a brick wall in a ruined district,
crushed together in the hands of midnight.

BROKEN ANGEL

It's raining down here.
Sonny Boy's up there on a cloud,
playing the blues harp.

THE LISTENER
for Godfrey Featherstone

He grew quieter in the last years,
walking slowly, the card of pain
kept hidden close to his chest;

drawing energy from stillness,
words chilled below zero to keep
their message clear and hard.

He knew the page was an instrument
for the hands and the breath;
he could read the score, but ached

for the improvised moment
when the cage door swung open
and the birds merged with the night.

NEMONYMOUS
for D.F. Lewis

I didn't know his name until afterwards:
retracing my steps, going back to his flat
with a note from the clinic, a reference number
translating magic into a sub-zero fact.

I didn't know her name until afterwards:
a social services record, a broken track
through the years. What did I expect?
One look at her posh house and I turned back.

I didn't know my name until afterwards:
after forty years of struggling, I was free
of men, women and booze. I was home again:
twenty thousand leagues under the sea.

THE NAKED EYE

Your sleep was so quiet
I thought you'd stopped breathing.
You'd stir only to get up
and add one more mug of water
to the row on the windowsill.

Your stillness marks the dull air
of my house, thumbnails of you
sitting hunched close to the fire,
leaning into the bathroom mirror,
watching me from the pillow.

Wherever I go I can't shut out
your lonely unwavering stare.
What planet were you looking for
in the night sky of my life,
above the fireworks and the smoke?

Now you're fitting a blind
to make your flat a darkroom.
Another world is jarring
towards clarity in your hands,
bruises marking its wet skin.

BLUE MOVIE

Bloken glass heaped in the jacuzzi,
blood turning mouldy on the pillow,
ice creeping up the satin sheets,

a single red tumour in a vase,
the stereo playing a death rattle,
soft lips flecked with white,

the hired limousine blown to dust,
a scream fading on the answerphone
and a text message, YOUR DEAD.

Strange that you can't stop watching
when it never makes you hard
and you tore up the picture.

RECORD

From the tracks, you can work it out.
The paths of two animals crossed,
and for part of a long night
they kept each other warm –

then continued on their ways,
leaving behind a narrow streak
where the snow had melted
in a shape they made together;

and now the water has refrozen
as black ice, a transparent sheet
that makes the road visible
as if saying: *It's time to go.*

THE MESSAGE

Halfway along Station Street
in the meltdown of closing time,

a mute prayer is given up
like a final showing of cards

or a nest of birds, startled,
trying to break from cover:

four rat-arsed, deaf soccer fans,
hands in the air, signing a chant.

THREE

CINEPHILIA
for John Lane

The last real favour I did for you
was to send you to that place.
A library of the black and white films
we'd seen together, decades ago,

in the Triangle or the Arts Lab:
flawed prints and pale subtitles –
Bergman, Tarkovsky, Wajda;
a depth of field behind the screen

where memory filtered a grey light
and the director was the author.
Now I sit in a darkened room
and see your life spread before me

as close as the wall, but beyond
my reach. I hear the playing
of a hoarse flute, see a man
stumbling lost in the blind tunnels.

NIGHTFALL

The TV shows a city of dark flames,
stealth bombers pounding a smoky waste.
I've walked out into a landscape
of turbulence frozen in passivity:
bare trees contorted by hard weather,
hidden birds like a radio's grey static;
one tree cut in half, the ground
littered with boughs and sections of trunk –
pale wood, shaved of bark, decaying.

Tonight it's four weeks since you died,
and we still can't plan the funeral
until the police have done more work;
and meanwhile, our masters are at war.
In this hollow, the darkness is pooling
and the streetlamps are coming closer,
bringing a faint imprint of your face.
I have to leave this exposed film
of cut-down trees and damaged survivors,

and go back into artificial light
where the news is still getting worse.
The birds are silent now, the picture
becoming its own torn silhouette,
and somehow I've been talking to you
and your message is only this:
there are no crows in the branches.
And it's too dark to go on writing,
but not too dark to find the way back.

UNBURIED

The field is crowded with ghosts –
distorted, shadowy, burning.
The light cracks in pools of oil,
the train has come to a dead stop.
There is no-one to build a bridge.

The lost struggle to remember
some fragment of what has been.
The mobile phones are screaming,
sunset touches the grass with fire
and your number is unobtainable.

Crows' nests have ruined the trees,
grey shapes are breeding in the soil.
The birds are wheeling in crazy triumph.
Sleeping pills can't hide the nightmares.
The TV screen's grinning continuity

can't finally stop us from seeing
the dismembered children, the blind
stirring in their blackened houses,
because there is nowhere to hide
and I wish that I could call you.

RECONSTRUCTION

It all comes back to this.
The black machines in the gutted house
burning petrol, releasing
an invisible scentless noose.
This time, safety inspectors stand by
with gas masks and CO meters.

Hours pass. The engines knock;
their breath makes the damp air shiver.
The inspectors note their readings,
maintain a human silence.
At the end, they take the machines away.
The cleaning of the house can begin.

FORENSIC

Not even in dreams, the flawless
drift of pure white snow
to hold the print or the bloodstain

like a sterile agar plate, a glass slide;
even in dreams, the mark is blurred
and the snow isn't clean enough.

The evidence thaws into newsprint
and the jury are not persuaded
and the mud clinging to the streets

might contain DNA or democracy,
but no-one can make it speak.
Reality is the same, but colder.

EDGE OF TOWN

'In a Springsteen track,' she said,
'you always get that moment
in the third verse when the backing
gets stronger, the mood darkens.
That's usually when he mentions his dad.'

The music fills the unlit room:
piano, drums, guitar; every instrument
beaten but not destroyed.
The moon shines its accidental light
on the bare road, the abandoned house.

LAST TRAIN

The train follows its invisible thread
through the maze of trees and cities
where the night scatters its armoury
of rain or bricks or hidden fire,
and freight trains hurtle like blind missiles

on routes that no-one is watching.
The inspector has clipped my ticket,
but where is the guard? The horn
blares. I squint at my reflection,
try to see another face.

LETTERS TO AN EMPTY HOUSE

The house is slowly falling apart.
The windows are smeared with dust,
photographs curl on the sideboard
and the hallway is choked with letters
you're unable to stop writing –

postcards from new countries,
gifts no-one has signed for,
and you still don't get the message:
it won't help to have the fax number,
it won't help to have the e-mail address,

if there's nobody living in the house
then your messages mean nothing.
You can load up a personal website,
you can put out your own newsletter
with all the things you have to say,

but the flaking of the damp plaster
and the creeping of the blind woodlice
will be the only sounds in the house,
and their echo in your unresolved dreams
will slowly evict you from your mind.

FIREWEED

It's all been cleared now, of course:
the ground flattened, divided by walls
and fences topped with razor-wire;
the weeds and rubbish burnt, ashes
mingled with grit and solutions.

They've taken up the tracks, crushed
the rusting cars, sprayed the fireweed,
burnt the mildewed chairs and beds
where adolescents had played house,
converted the waste land to property.

Places like that breed crime, especially
in late summer. The rain-pools stink
and the flares of red blossom let go
of their white seed-fibres. The thicker
the smoke, the brighter the flame bleeds.

Don't go back. It's a trading estate
now, a barred and cost-effective space
watched over by guard dogs. Besides,
when you're trying to rebuild, you don't need
a place that was ruined to start with.

THE TERMINUS

You know the moment you walk in.
Madness echoes in the long corridors,
the invisible vaults, the tunnels.
The air crackles with the sound of rain.

Once admitted, you peer at the screens
for your destination, then hurry down
to some crowded platform. The others:
guided by earplugs, clutching dolls,

talking angrily to themselves.
The static congeals into a voice
you can't understand, but the others
think it means a platform change

and you run with them, upstairs
and down again, fumbling with cases.
Still nothing comes. In the grey light
you scan the obsolete timetable.

Back among the guards, you demand
the train you came for. Blank looks,
shaken heads. "There's a meeting."
You're shown the bars across the door,

warned not to cause more trouble.
"You're free to leave, but if you try
to go, we'll detain you." You walk
alone down the frozen escalator,

shaking with rage – just in time
to see the train go through like a fist,
its windows dark, its metallic teeth
grinding. The tunnels shudder.

VANILLA HELL

Time came back. I could feel
how three years had dropped away
while I paced the same rooms,
spraying the dead air with vanilla.

Space came back. I could see
the crater in the living-room floor
I'd been walking round, covering up
the damage with a vanilla rug.

You came back. I could hear you
in my head, for the first time
in three years of holding a telephone
that always smelt of vanilla.

Now I breathe traffic fumes
and drink bitter coffee. My dreams
coat my mouth with bile.
It's worse. It's so much better.

RAIN

All through the winter, you didn't get
one night's unbroken sleep.
But now the rain is falling:
it settles its folds around you
like the rust of an untreated wound.

There's a hollow in the bed your shape.
The downpour is washing away
the democratic threats, the soundbite vomit,
the brutal politeness of the courtroom.
The dead leaves have turned to shit.

Draw the curtain, don't answer the phone.
Let the rain erase facts, voices, streets,
until there's nothing left but static:
the placebo of a world without tears.
Sleep a week, a season. Sleep for years.

PERMANENT REVOLUTION

Six rusty strings corrode the sky.
October's winds are tearing up the world
and patching together a better one;

and there's a taste in my mouth
of whisky, smoke, blood and tinfoil,
bandages from a hidden wound.

The paints are dissolving in the rain;
every colour is tinged with red.
This slow destruction feels like healing.

Another day, a stained copper coin
whose sides are memory and forgetting.
There's no easy way to get through.

NEVER AGAIN

It starts with the paperwork:
gathering the scattered documents
of birth and citizenship,
writing the death certificates,
hanging the blackened leaves
on the skeleton of a family tree.

Then sifting through the rubble
for the teeth of children,
washing the tattered clothes.
The ash gets under your skin,
the structures of ruined houses
hold your dreams prisoner.

Say it. You might feel better.
Like an alcoholic coming round
and muttering the classic promise.
The worst thing is, you mean it.
But the future is a building made up
of unfurnished rooms, each one a never.

PLUTO

Can you cry away your sight?
The doctor talks to you about retinas,
leaking blood vessels, histological
madness. "We'll keep looking at it."
You walk out into the platinum blaze
of an August day. The light shakes you
like a headline you can't ignore.
You should have worn sunglasses.
By the time you reach home, the sun
has pulled you into outer space.
You're crying once more, without feeling.
Indoors, you draw all the curtains
and lie on the bed, keeping still,
thinking about the ninth planet.

REBELS' REST

They never came to a bad end,
all those trouble-makers, agitators,
rebels, saboteurs, malcontents.
Some had the fight knocked out,
got paid off, or simply gave up.

Some never quit the barricades,
tasting the slow diabetes of failure
in how much of a threat they weren't
to a world where the word 'new'
was in every mouth, like Prozac.

They still live in the future,
still wait for the dawn of reason,
still walk the unchanged streets
as if a spring thaw were coming
to melt the buildings and fences,

move the still blood in hearts
told it's their nature not to beat.
The chant of ignorance pursues them,
a static flooding the bare city
where they were born and erased.

ONE MORE TIME

This train doesn't cross bridges,
it goes under them.
I'm sitting with my back
to the engine, watching the trees
slowly tear themselves away –

peroxide fields, a grey factory
turned inside-out, a bridge
where a rope has hung for nine
years; this journey I made
twice every working day.

A narrow Virgin train
whips past like a deadline.
On one side of it, the faces
still talking; on the other side,
the things they have said.

PRESUMED DEAD

If they come back – from the wastes of alcohol,
obscurity or madness – they come back alone.
Their scars masked by oddly placed silences
or facial hair. A blankness in their eyes
that their smiles never touch, from when
they hit the roadblock of middle age at ninety
miles an hour, like Kowalski in *Vanishing Point*.
Sometimes clutching an unpublished book, a personal
organiser, or (God help us all) a new faith.

You're glad to see them, at first. They outlive
the comeback, start trying to settle scores;
turn up at Party meetings with documents
you need tunnel vision to read; lose the same
battles they lost the first time, but harder.
This time they're in it for the duration: taut
and acrid, hand-rolled, always gleaming
with the failure that clings to them like gelatine
on the cheapest tinned meat, a version of spam.

THE LANDSLIDE
for Simon Bestwick

The view came suddenly. From grey walls
heavy with stored rain, a cobbled street
ended in a broken ledge –
then a slope overgrown with moss
and trees, old bricks in their roots.
A disaster frozen by permanence,
or as much of it as we understand.

Unable to keep our pace steady,
we scrambled down through the ruins
to the dull plasma of the Irwell,
hardly flowing. We walked for an hour
across tracks and mud-crusted fields
to where a new chain-link fence
caught the last light, blocked our way.

As we cast around for directions
in a fading wilderness, our minds
were on those buried in their houses
by missiles, bulldozers or hope.
Tired now, limping and subdued,
we made it back to the road
before darkness emptied the wide valley.

TEXT

After the crash, they buried that kid
with a phone in his intact hand,
so his friends could text him:

words ghosted on the screen
in a virtual book of condolences,
a dark page held down by stones.

COMEBACK

Not so much a talking cure
as a way to listen –

like rebreaking an arm
healed out of shape,

opening a skylight
in the roof of the sky.

Standing by the doorway,
hearing the raven

flap its wings outside,
the steady beat of darkness.

Knowing it has more
than one word to say.

BIOGRAPHICAL NOTE

JOEL LANE's two previous collections of poems, *The Edge of the Screen* and *Trouble in the Heartland*, are both published by Arc. His other work includes two novels, *From Blue to Black* and *The Blue Mask*; a novella, *The Witnesses Are Gone*; and three collections of short stories, *The Earth Wire*, *The Lost District* and *The Terrible Changes*.

He lives in Birmingham, where he works as a journalist and enjoys long walks, urban landscapes, cinemas and bookshops. His happiest hours have been spent offline.

Recent titles in Arc Publications'
POETRY FROM THE UK / IRELAND include:

LIZ ALMOND
The Shut Drawer
Yelp!

JONATHAN ASSER
Outside The All Stars

DONALD ATKINSON
In Waterlight: Poems New,
Selected & Revised

ELIZABETH BARRETT
A Dart of Green and Blue

JOANNA BOULTER
Twenty Four Preludes & Fugues on
Dmitri Shostakovich

JAMES BYRNE
Blood / Sugar

THOMAS A CLARK
The Path to the Sea

TONY CURTIS
What Darkness Covers
The Well in the Rain

JULIA DARLING
Sudden Collapses in Public Places
Apology for Absence

CHRIS EMERY
Radio Nostalgia

LINDA FRANCE
You are Her

KATHERINE GALLAGHER
Circus-Apprentice
Carnival Edge

CHRISSIE GITTINS
Armature

RICHARD GWYN
Sad Giraffe Café

MICHAEL HASLAM
The Music Laid Her Songs in Language
A Sinner Saved by Grace
A Cure for Woodness

MICHAEL HULSE
The Secret History

BRIAN JOHNSTONE
The Book of Belongings

JOEL LANE
Trouble in the Heartland

HERBERT LOMAS
The Vale of Todmorden
A Casual Knack of Living
(COLLECTED POEMS)

PETE MORGAN
August Light

MICHAEL O'NEILL
Wheel

MARY O'DONNELL
The Ark Builders

IAN POPLE
An Occasional Lean-to

PAUL STUBBS
The Icon Maker

SUBHADASSI
peeled

LORNA THORPE
A Ghost in My House

MICHELENE WANDOR
Musica Transalpina
Music of the Prophets

JACKIE WILLS
Fever Tree
Commandments